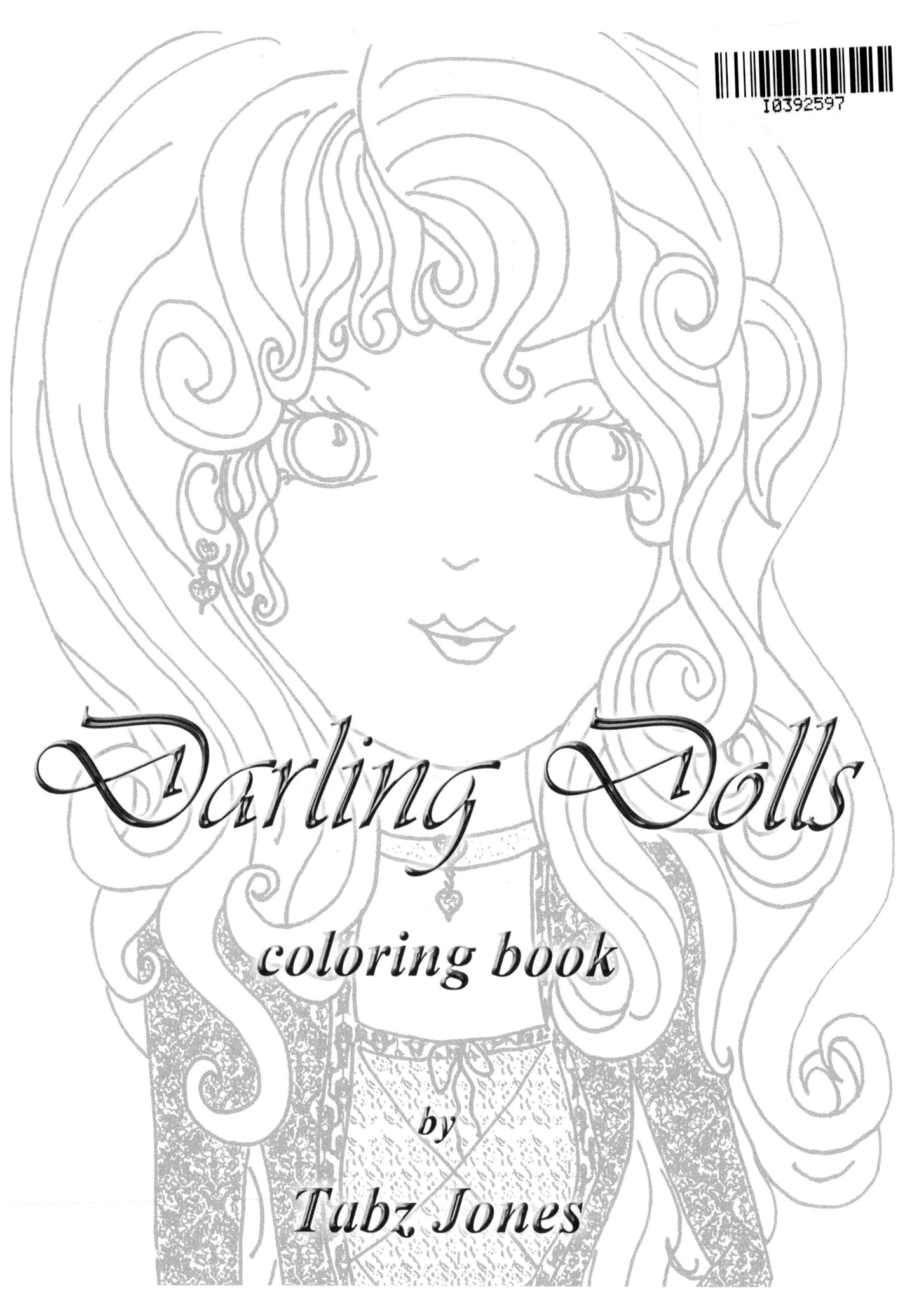

Darling Dolls

coloring book

by

Tabz Jones

Other Books by Tabz Jones

Digital Landscape Adult Coloring Book

Fantasy Art Mini Adult Coloring Book

Sun and Sand Adult Coloring Book

Gothic Fairy Dream Journal

Rockabilly Roses Journal

Dark Matter Adult Coloring Book

Angelic Book of Shadows

Dangerous Curves Adult Coloring Book

Fantasy Men Adult Coloring Book

Harlequinn Pastel Fantasy Dream Journal

Gothiscopic Kaleidoscopes Coloring Book

Gothic Girls Adult Coloring Book Volumes 1-5

Steampunk Adult Coloring Book

Fantasy Fae Adult Coloring Book

Fractal Art Adult Coloring Book Volumes 1-2

In Loving Memory Churchyard Adult Coloring Book

Fantasy Art Adult Coloring Book Volumes 1-2

Doodle Monsters Adult Coloring Book

Summer Flowers Adult Coloring Book

Skullz Adult Coloring Book Volumes 1-2

Rose Cross Dream Journal

Dark Fantasy Adult Coloring Book Volumes 1-3

Classic Swears Adult Coloring Book Standard and Mini Editions

Statuesque Adult Coloring Book

Reflections Vampire Poetry

Printed in the United States of America

First Printing, 2016

ISBN-13:
978-1535332705

ISBN-10: 1535332700

Tabz Jones

PO BOX 2137

Alma AR 72921

www.gothictoggs.net

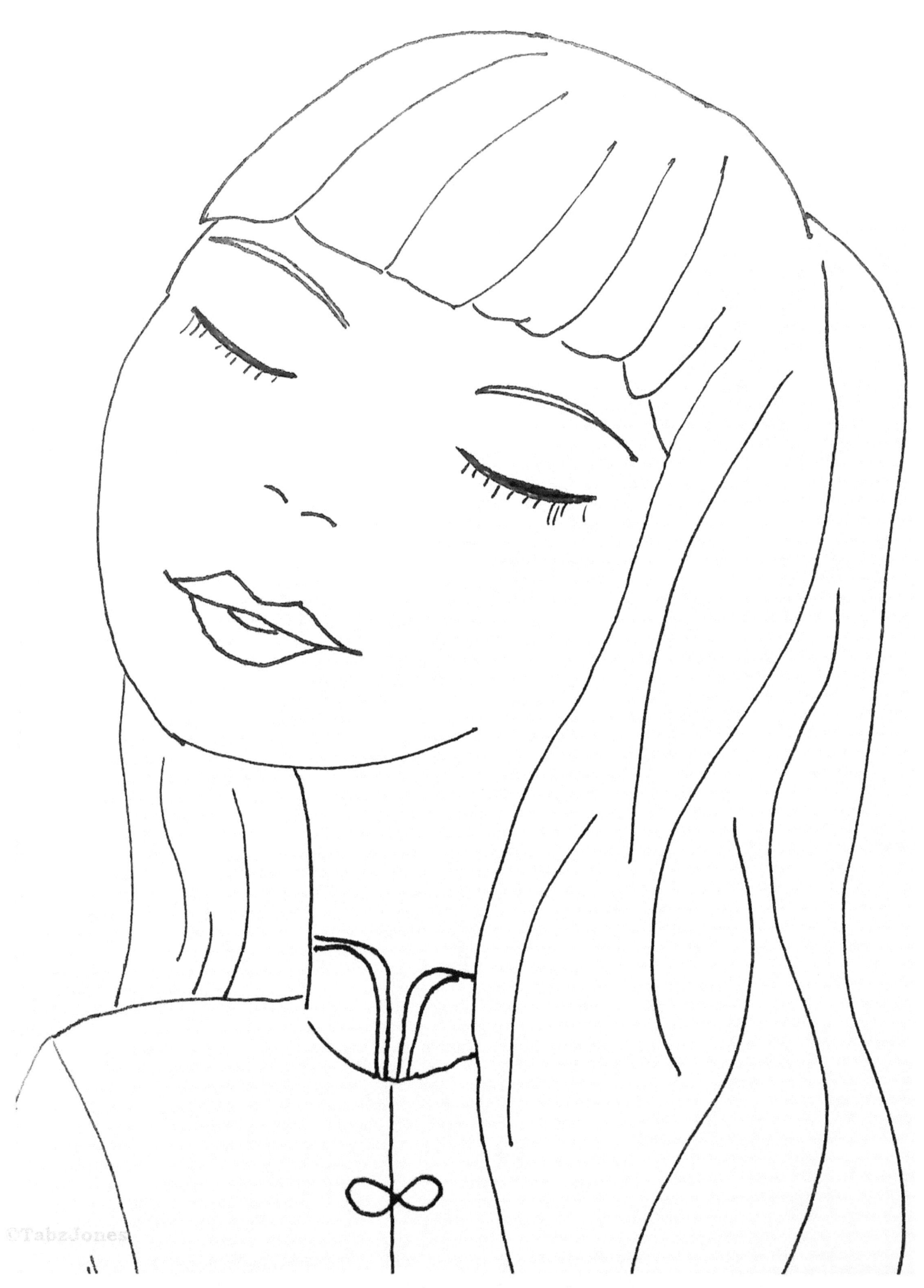

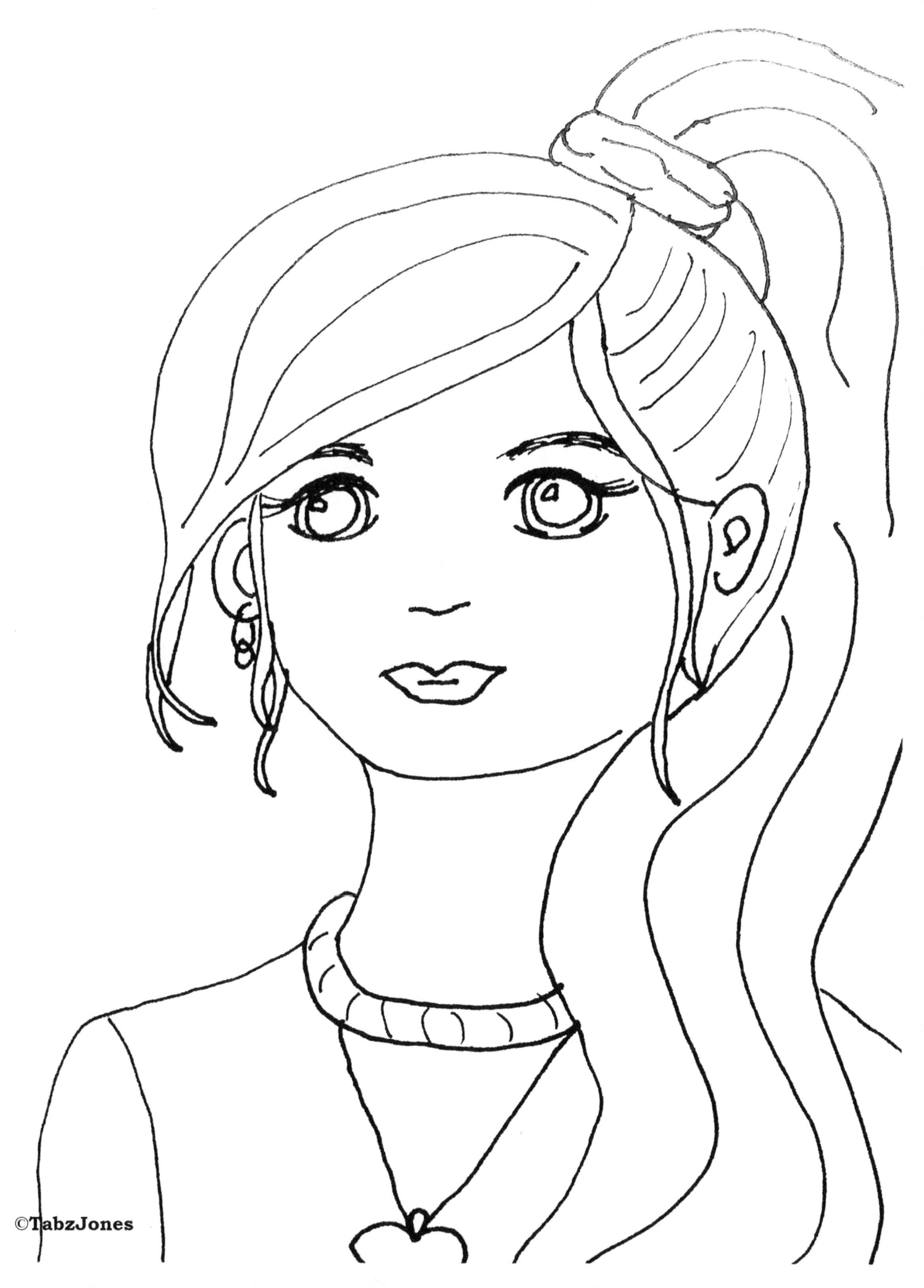

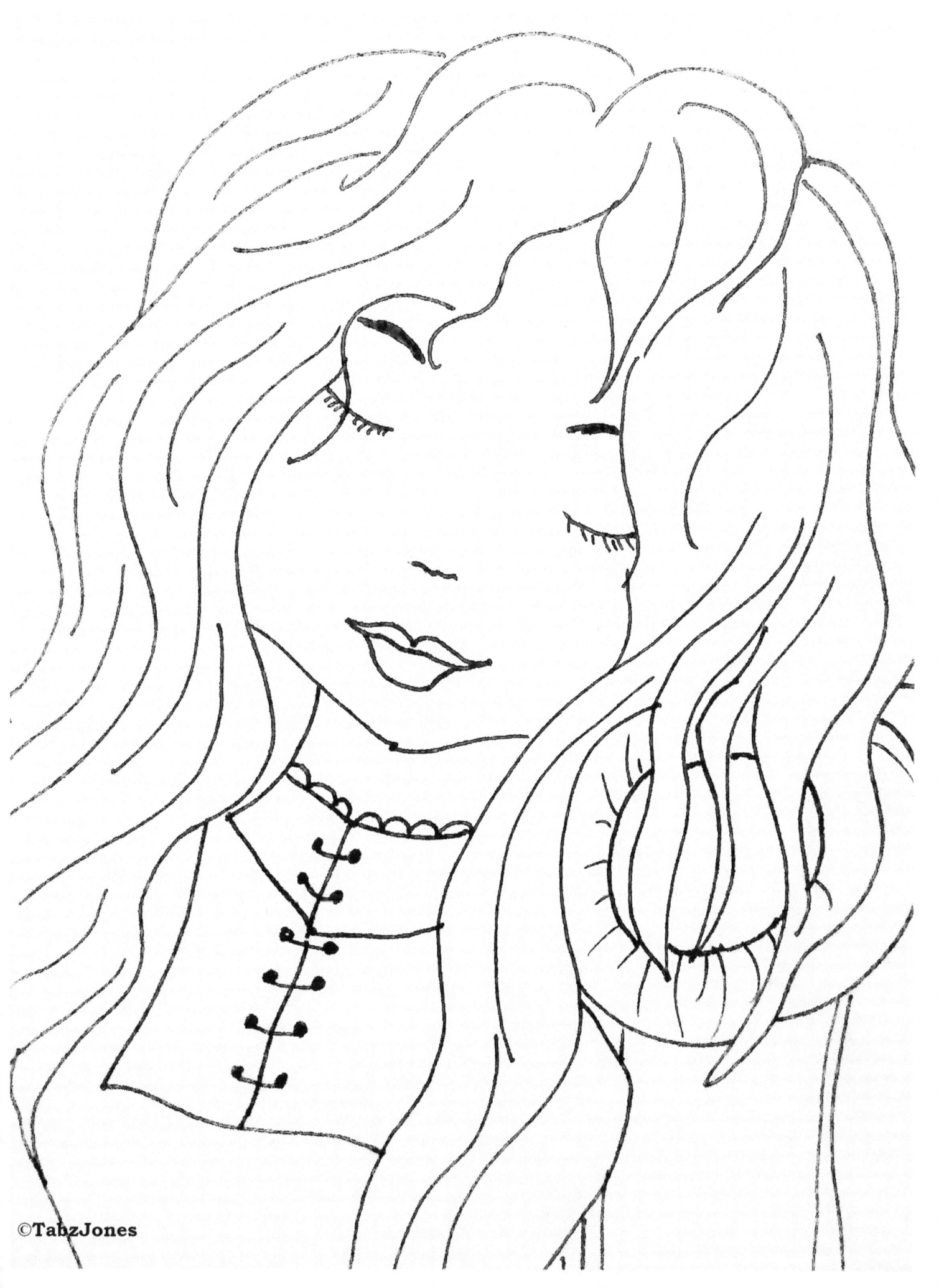

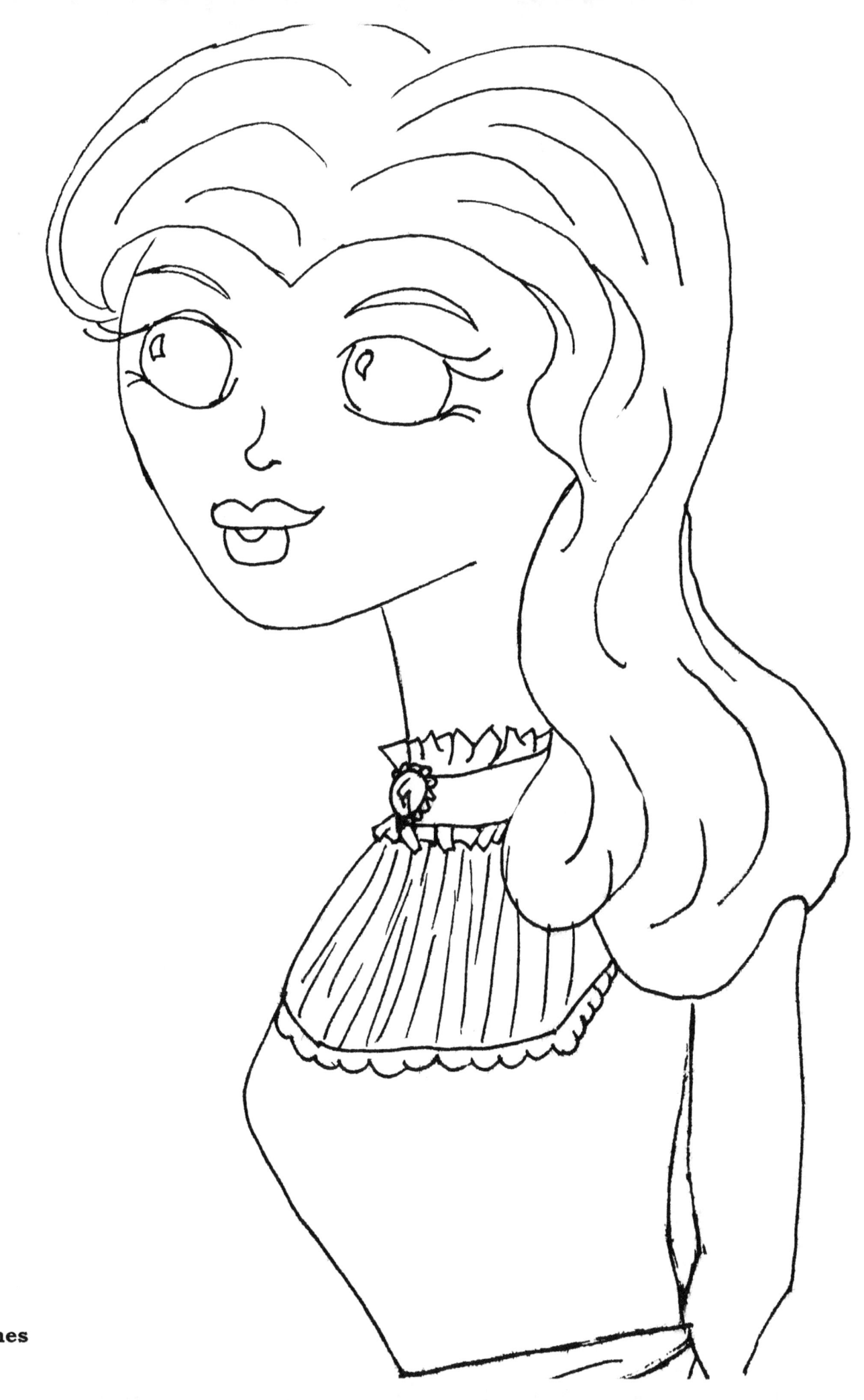

©TabzJones

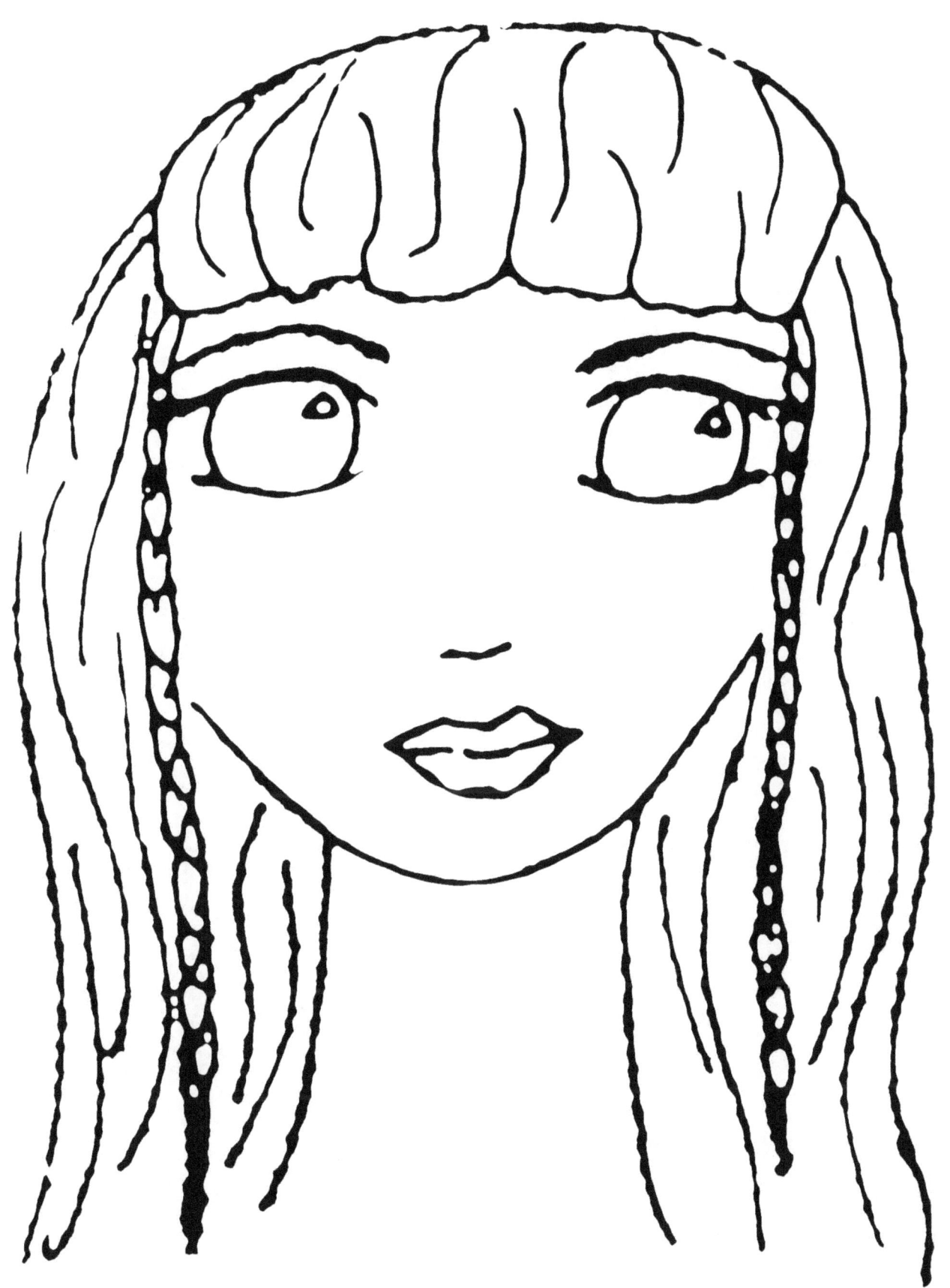

©TabzJones

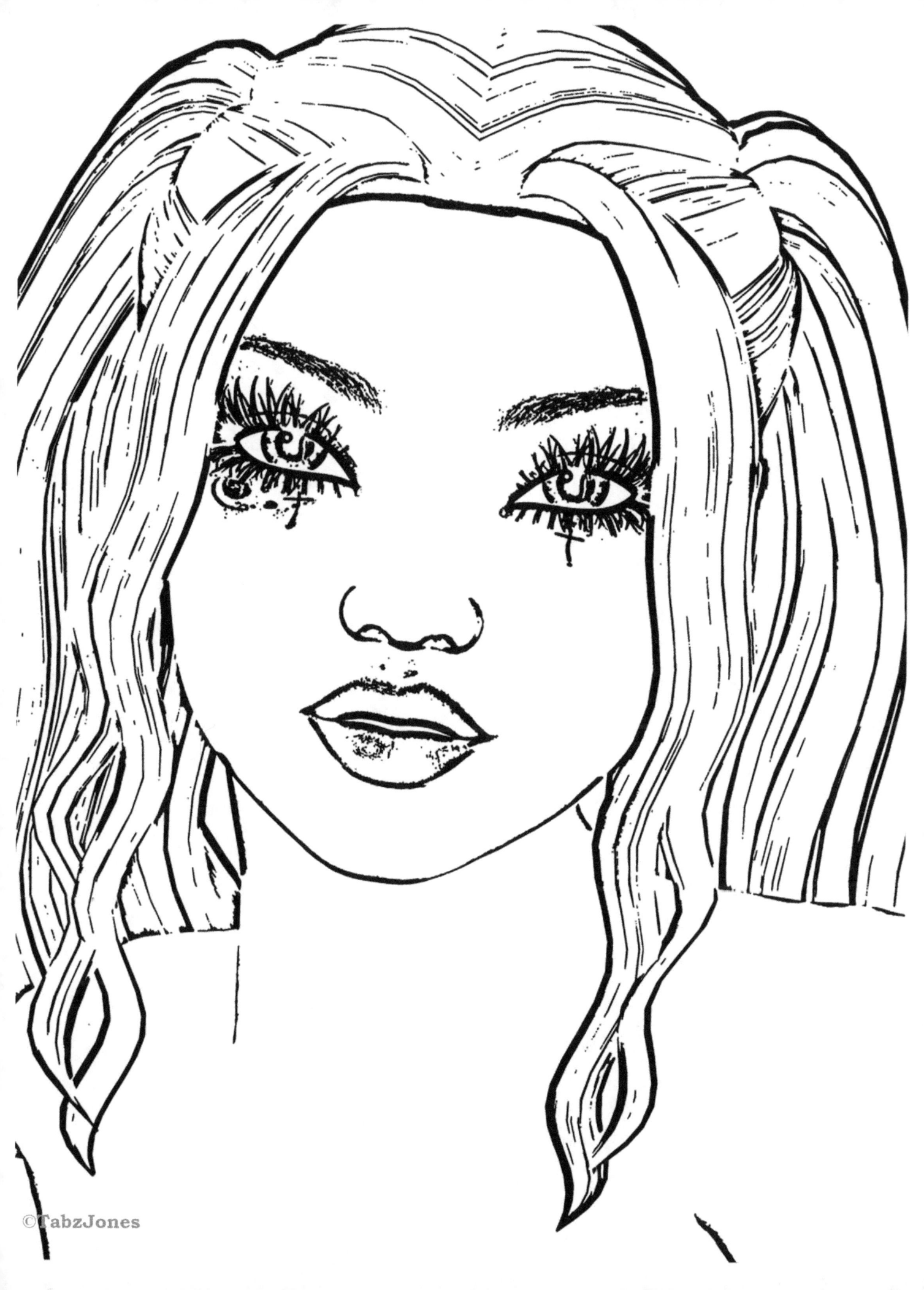

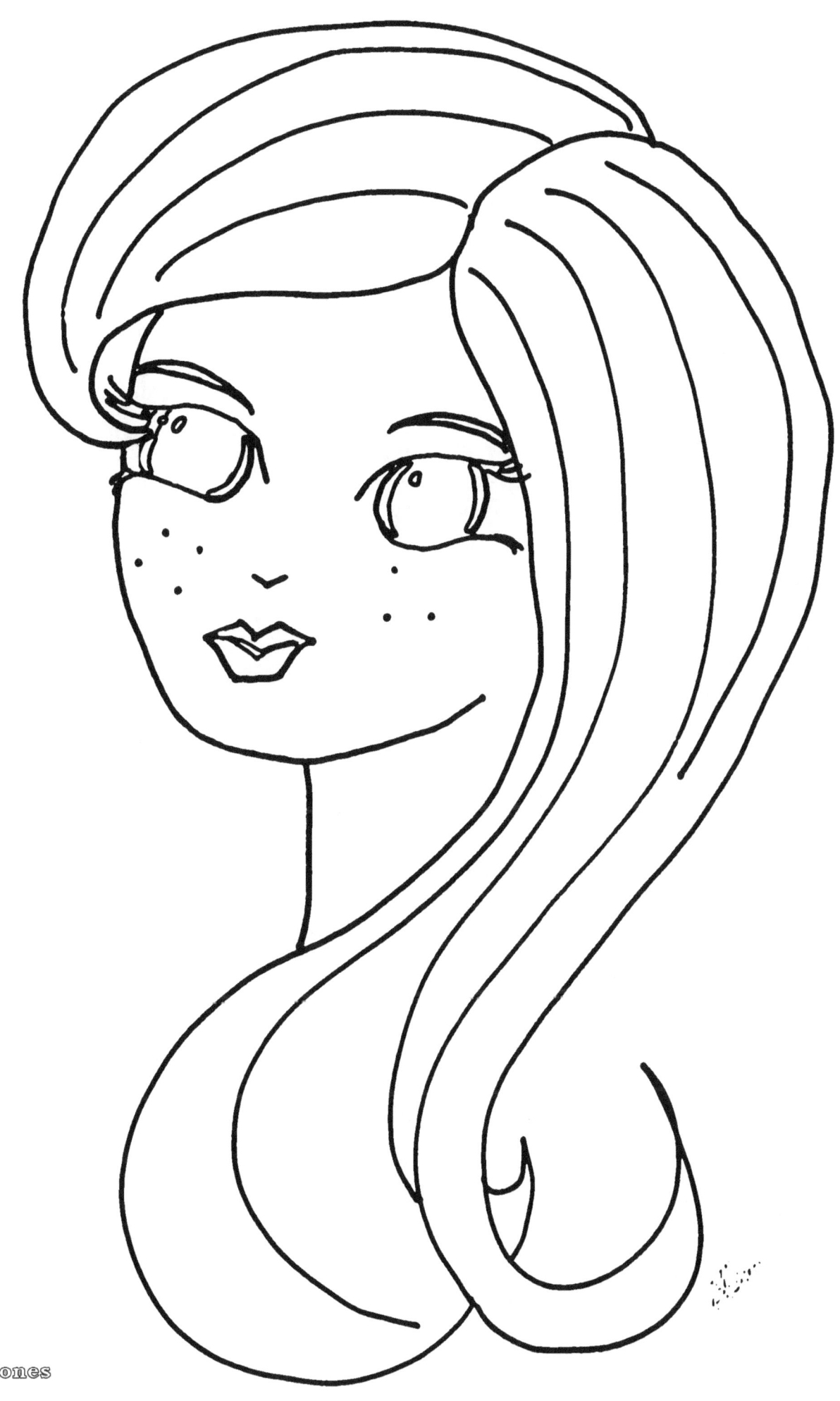

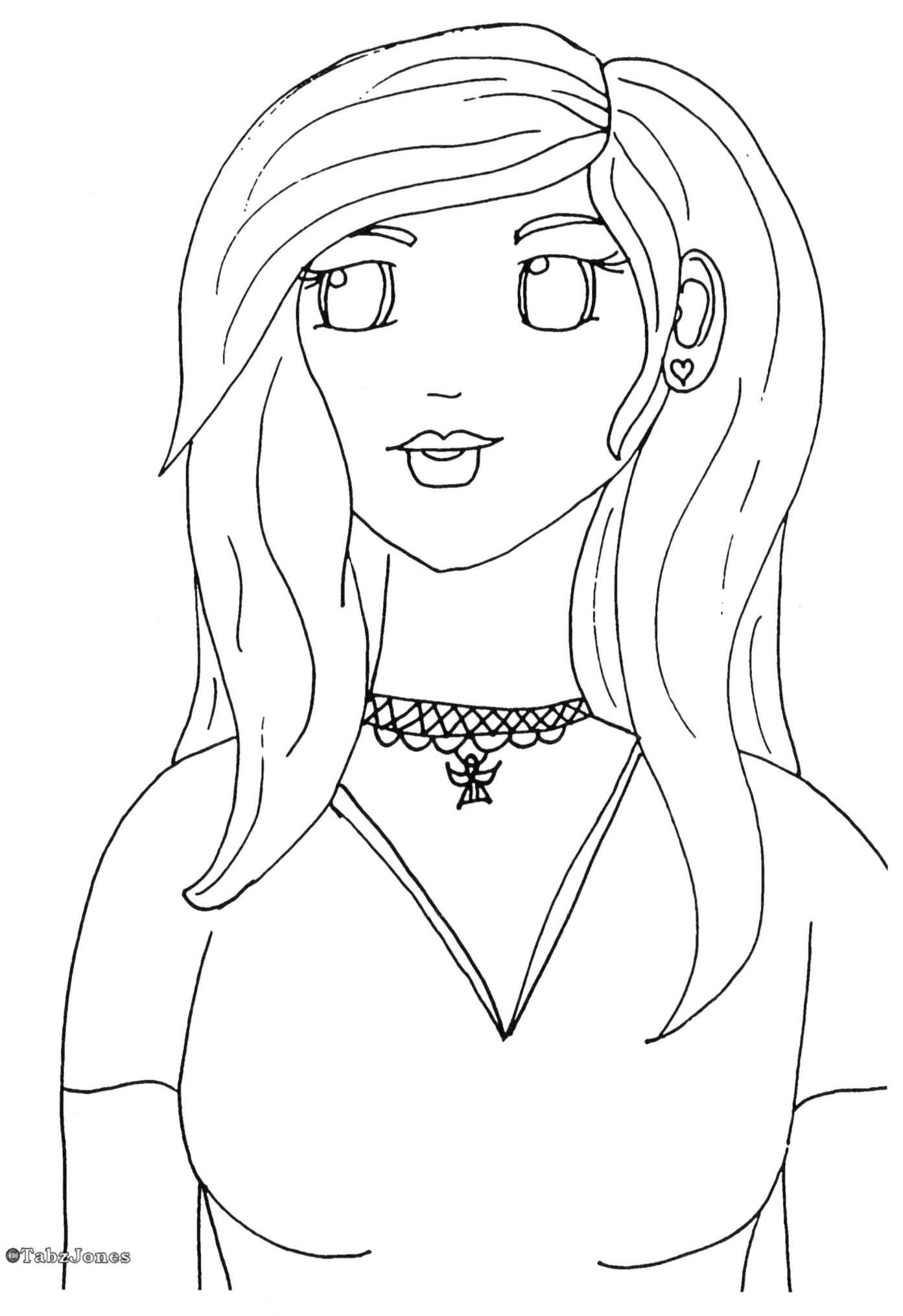

©TabzJones

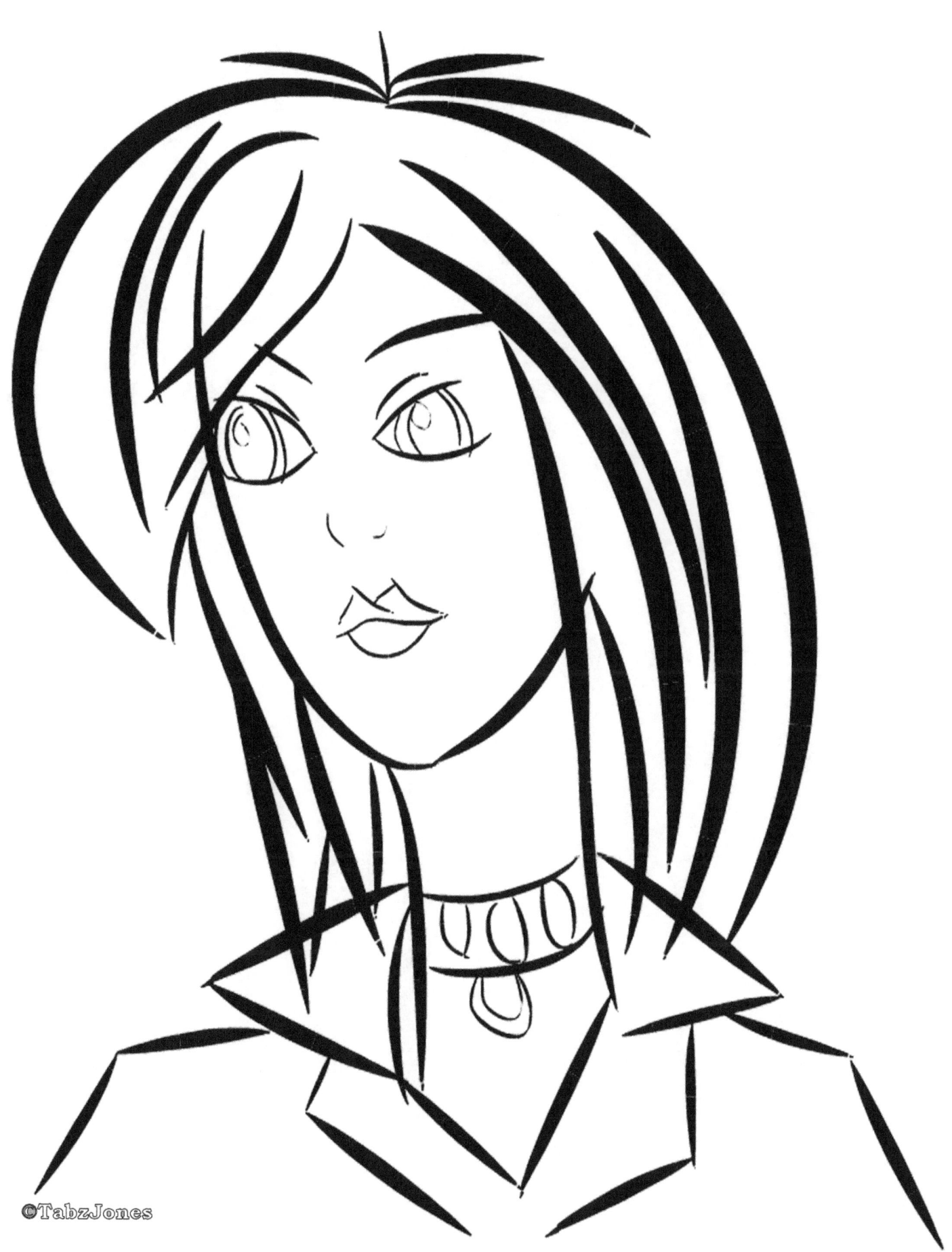

©TabzJones

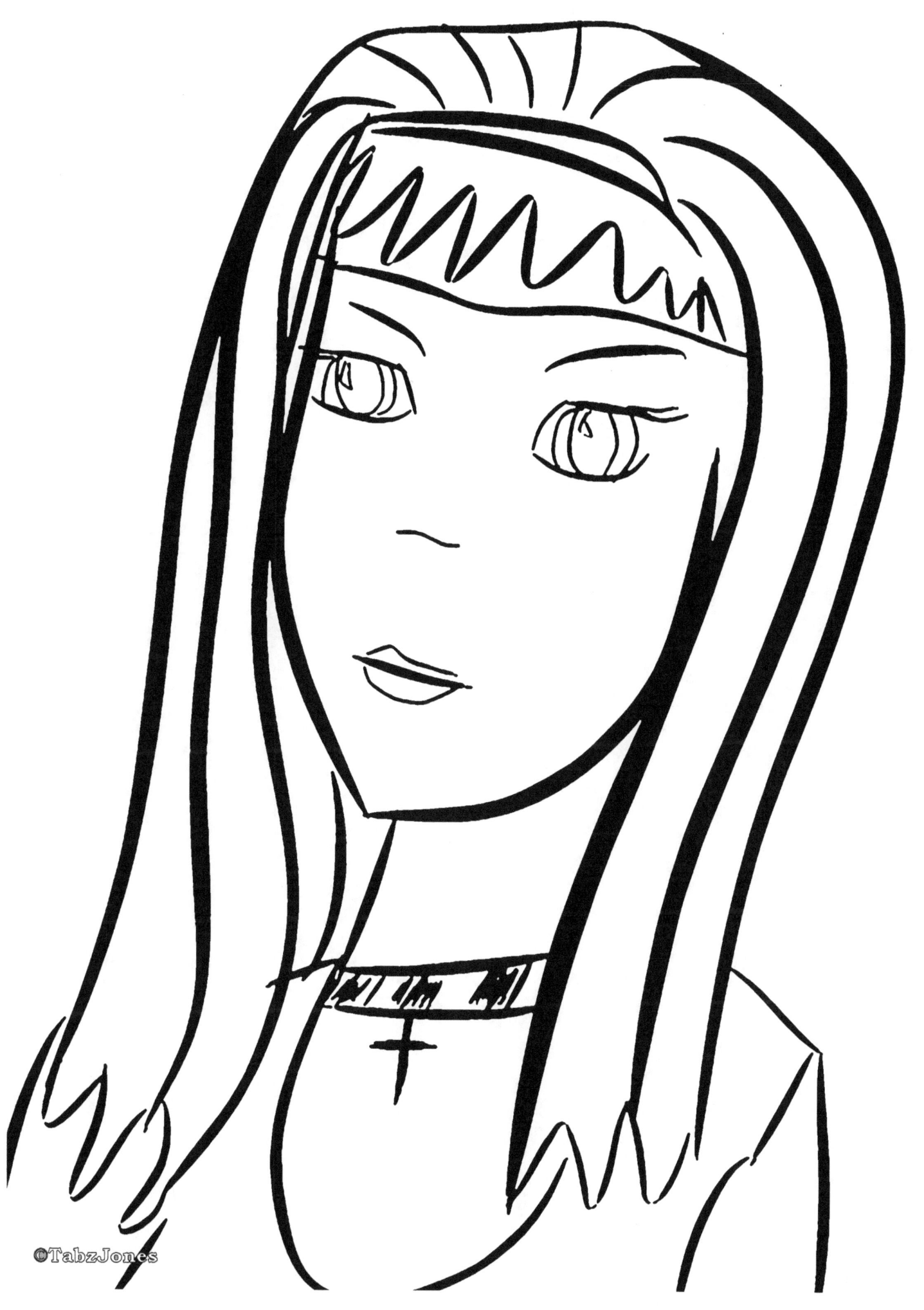
©TabzJones

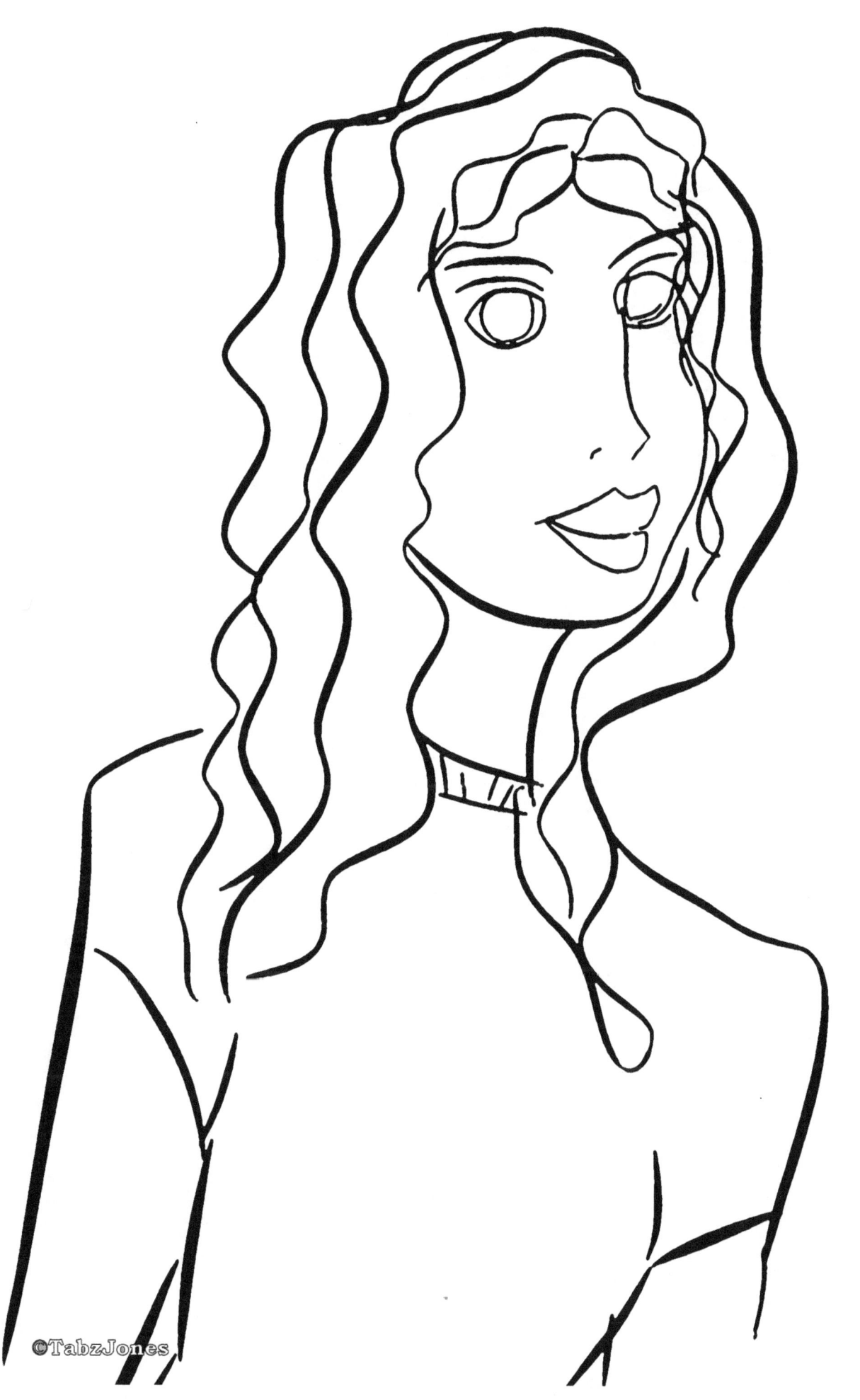

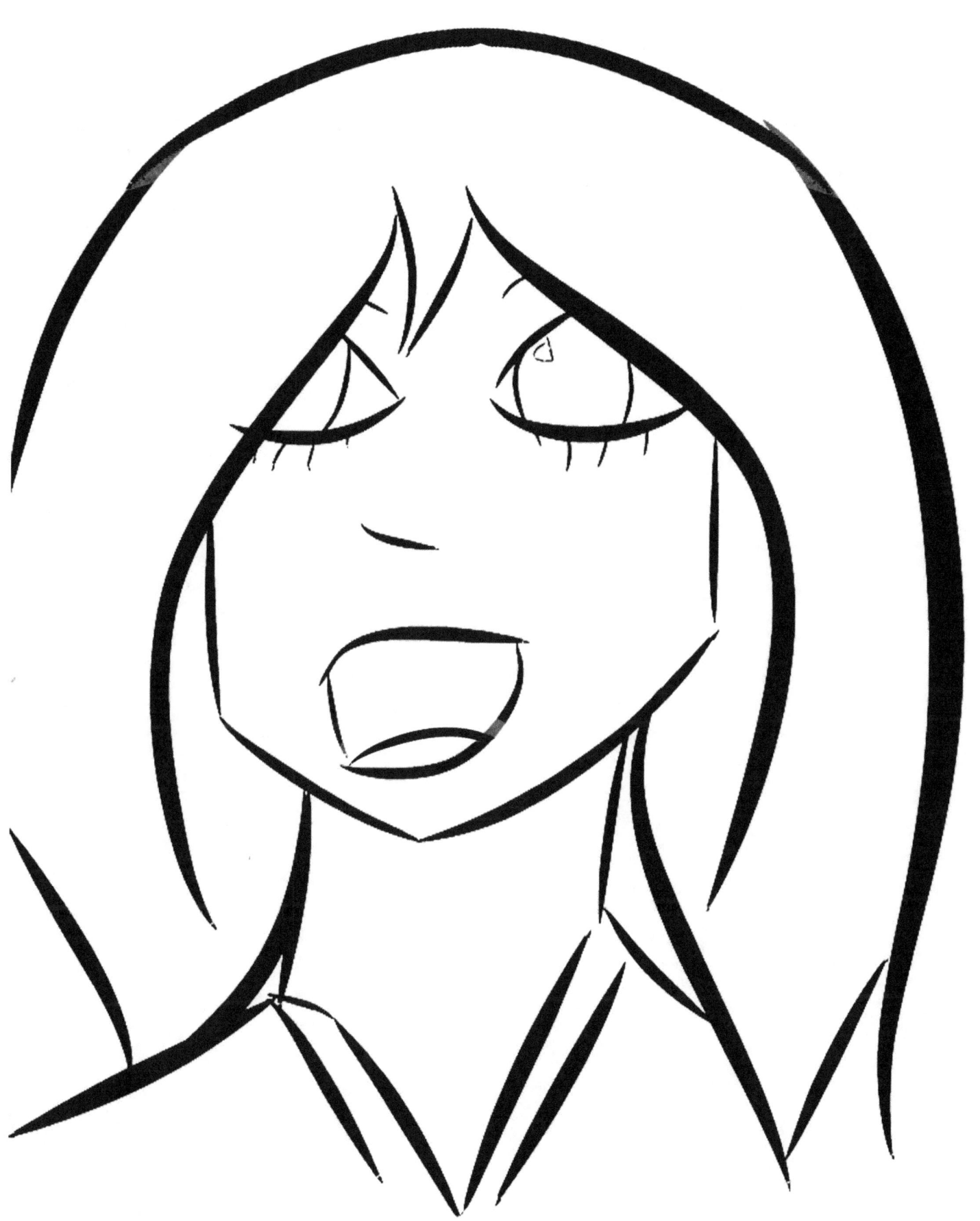

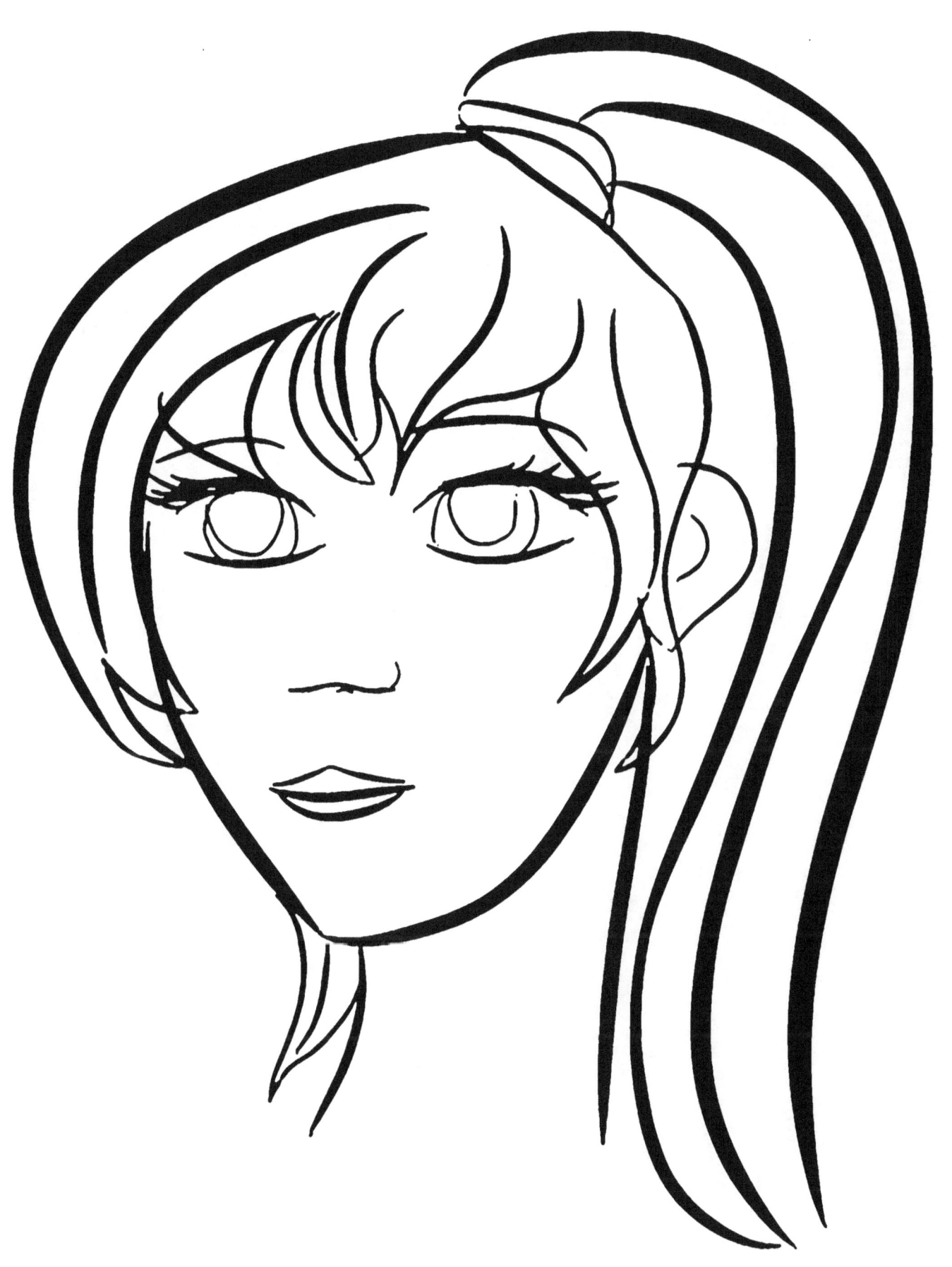
©TabzJones

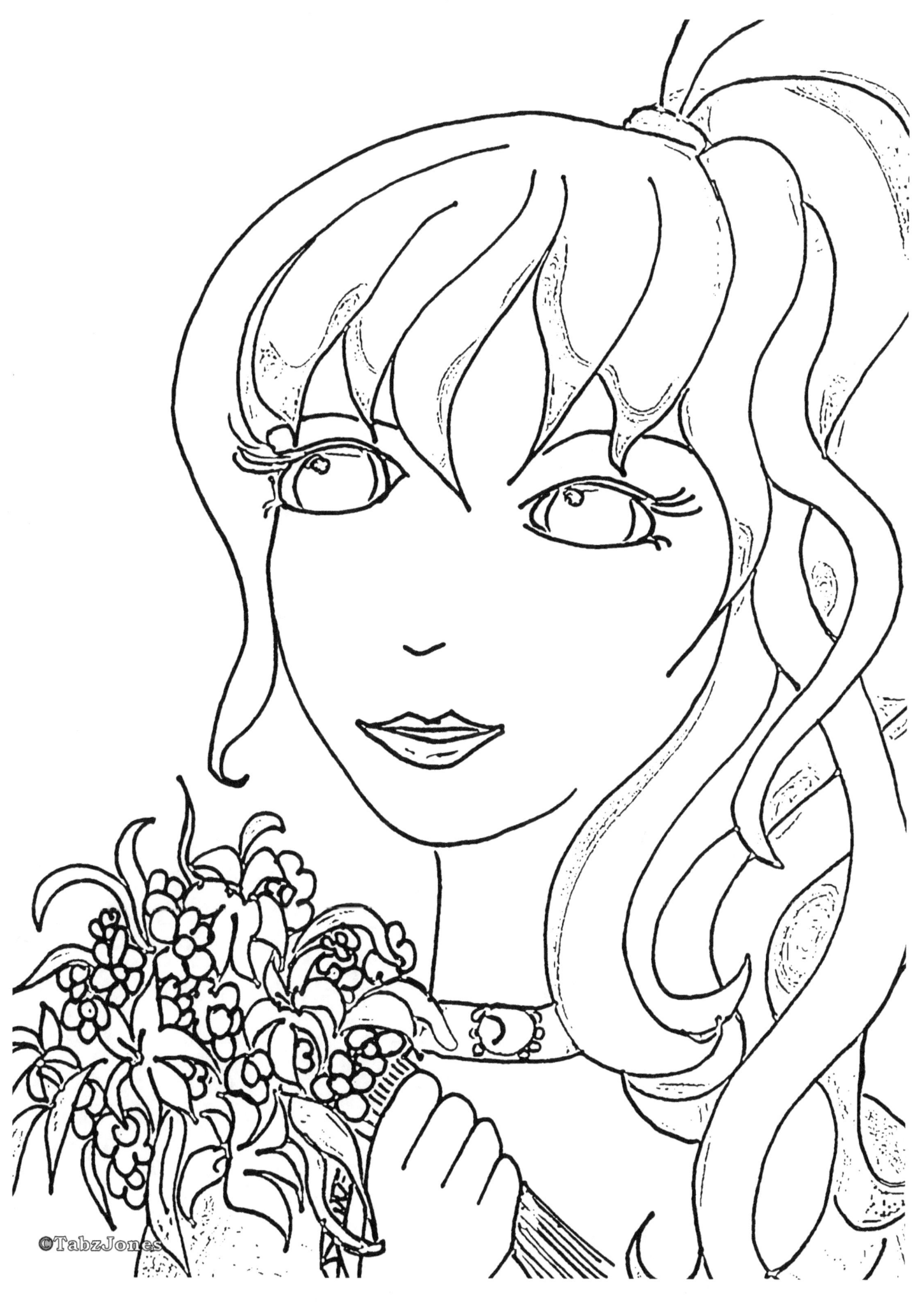

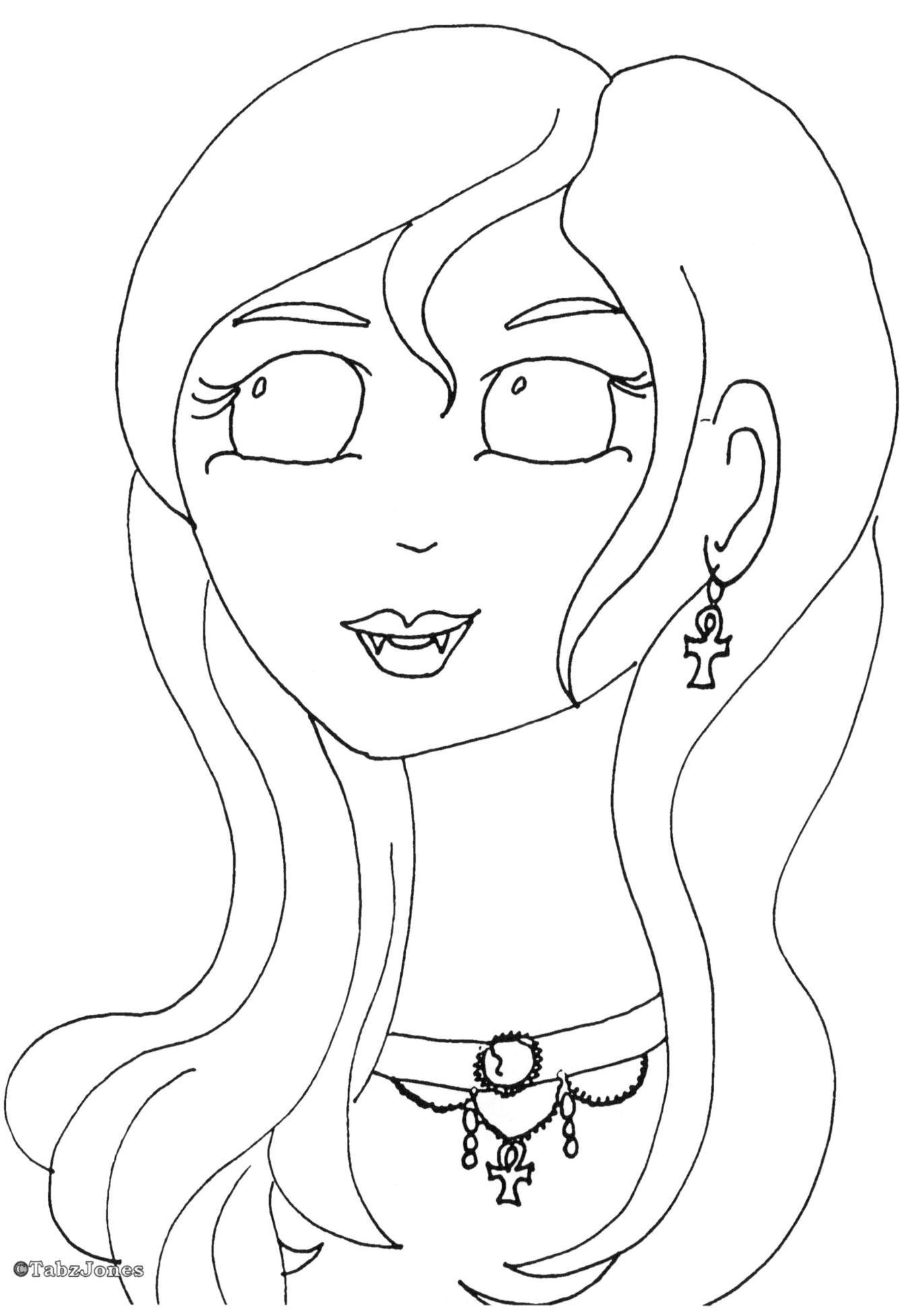

©TabzJones

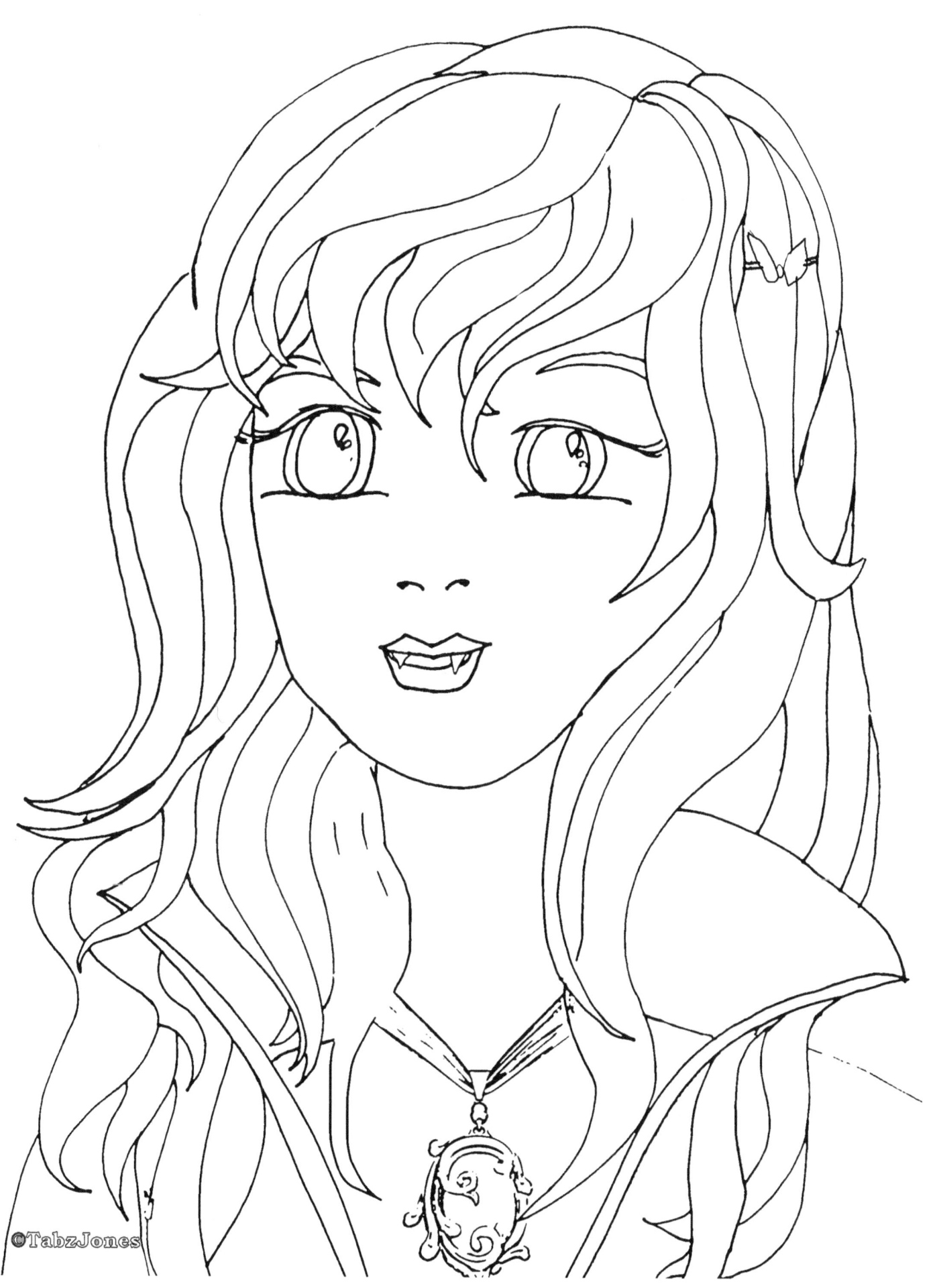
©TabzJones

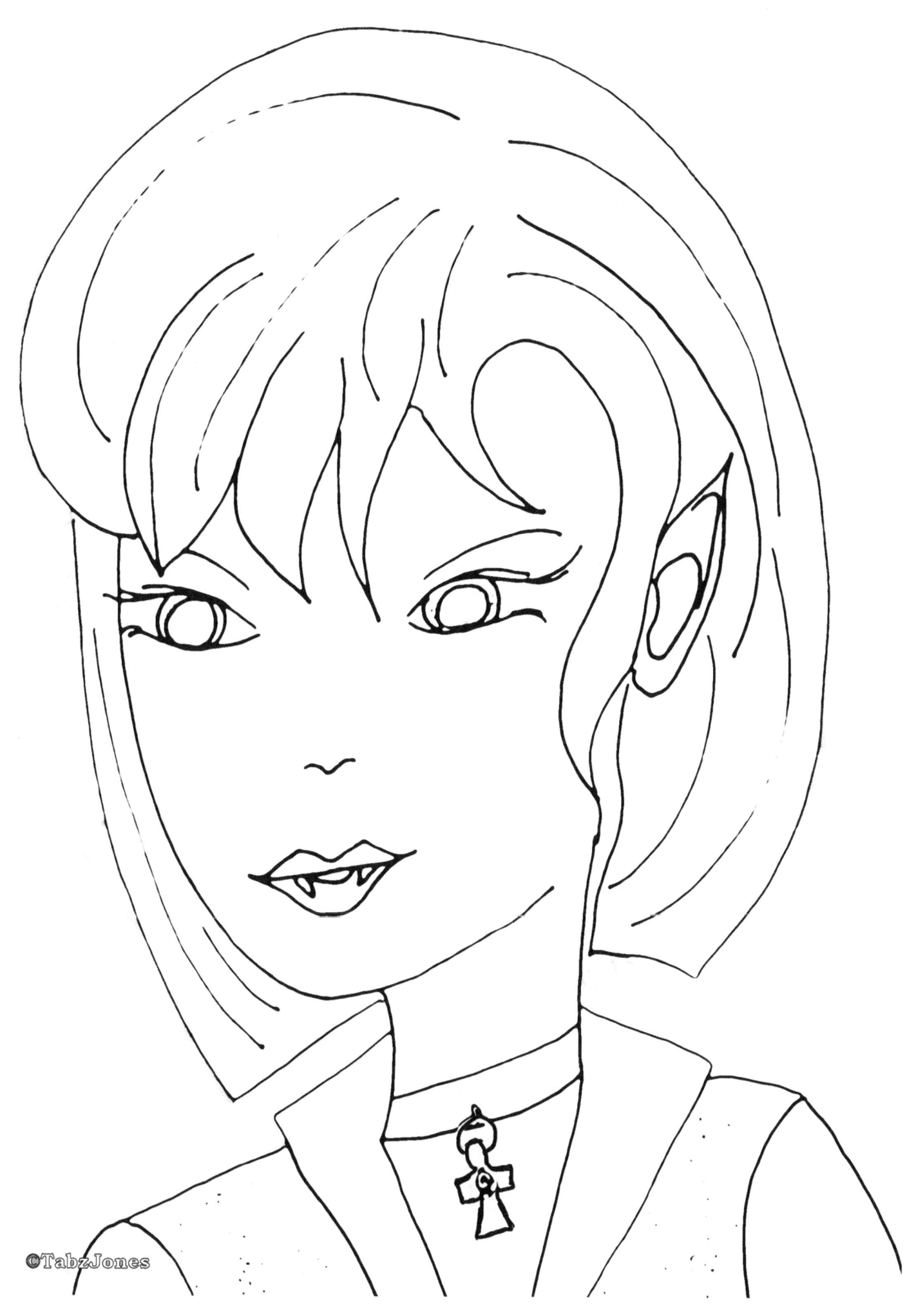

©TabzJones

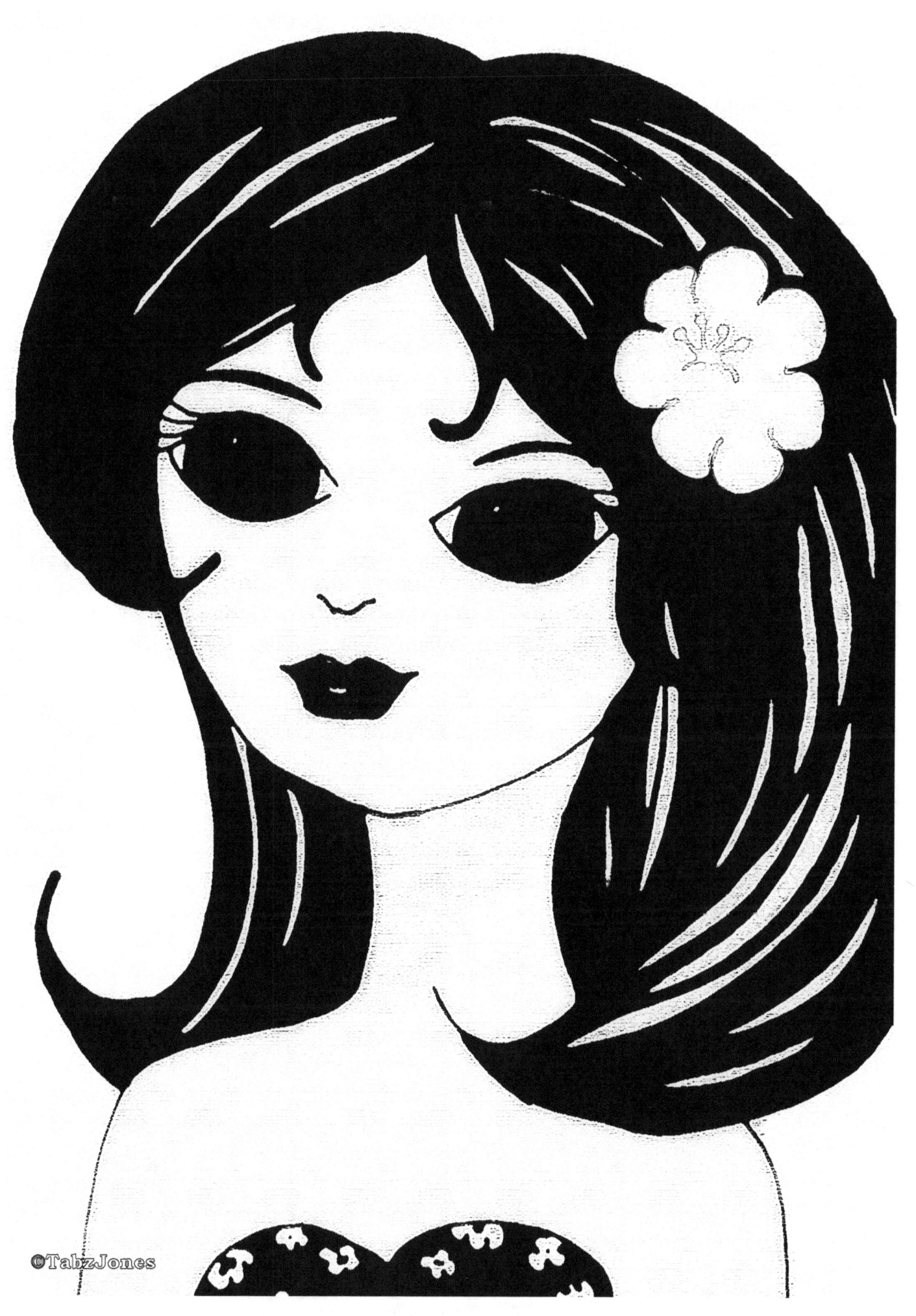

©TabzJones

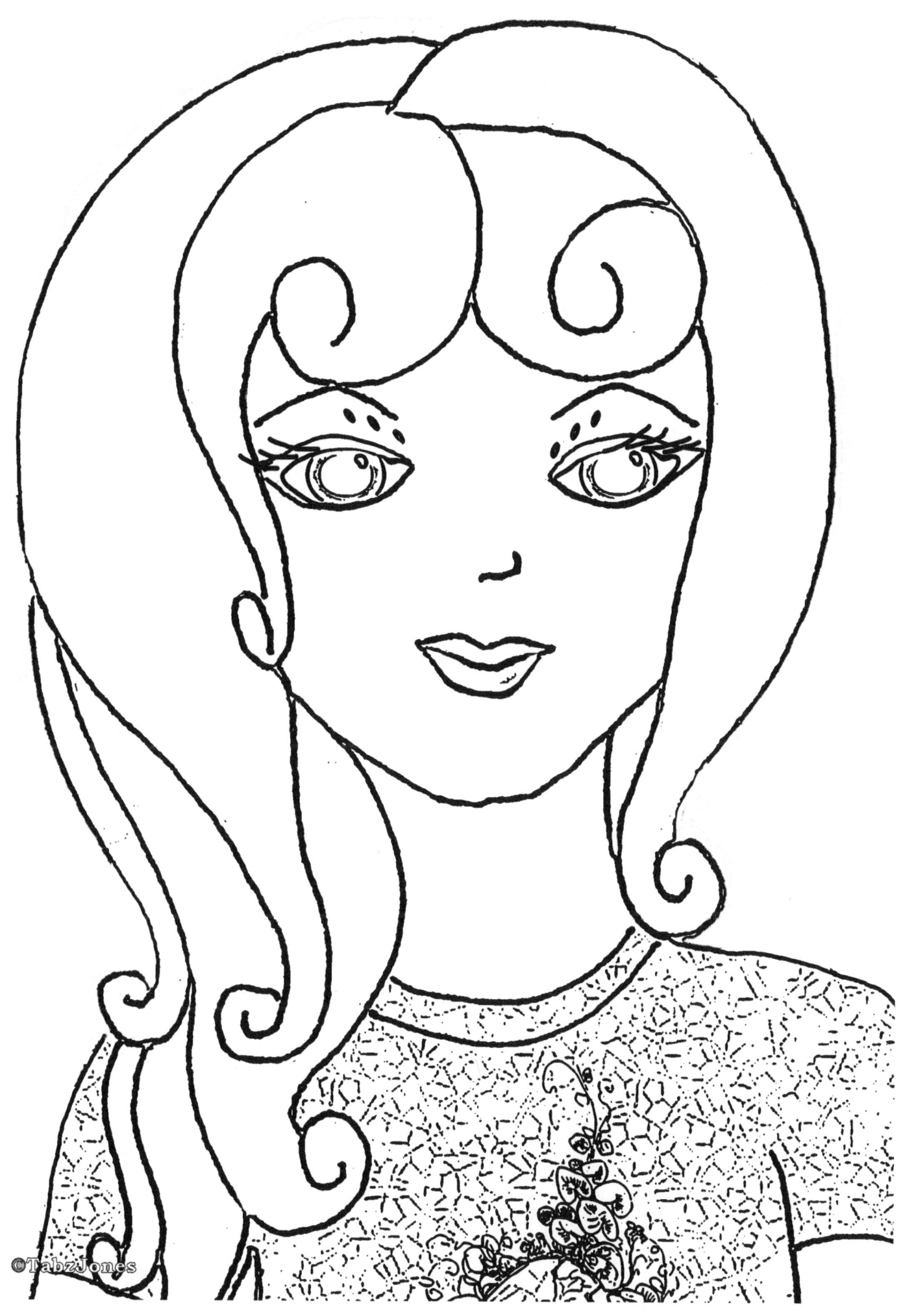

©TabzJones

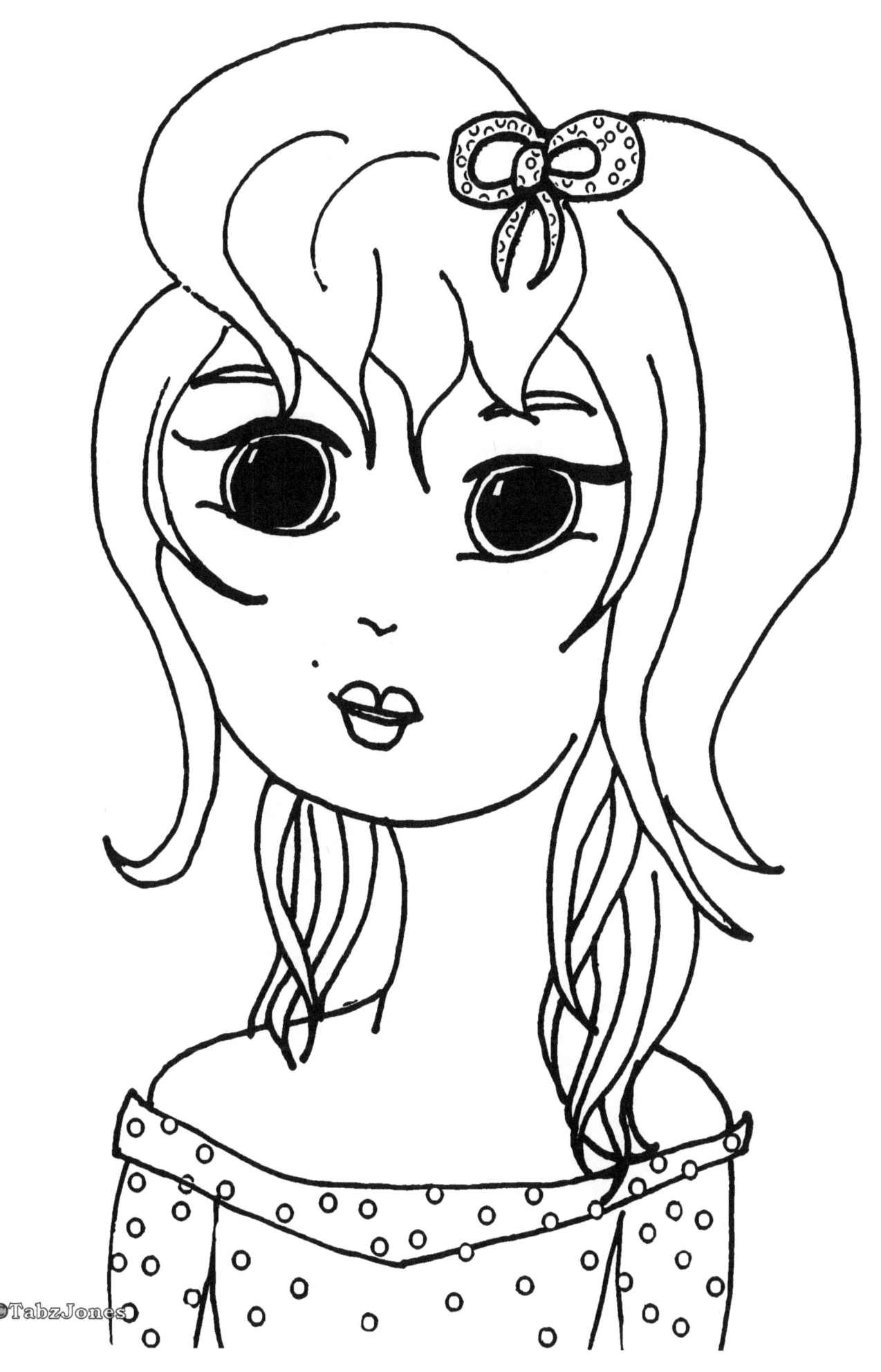
©TabzJones

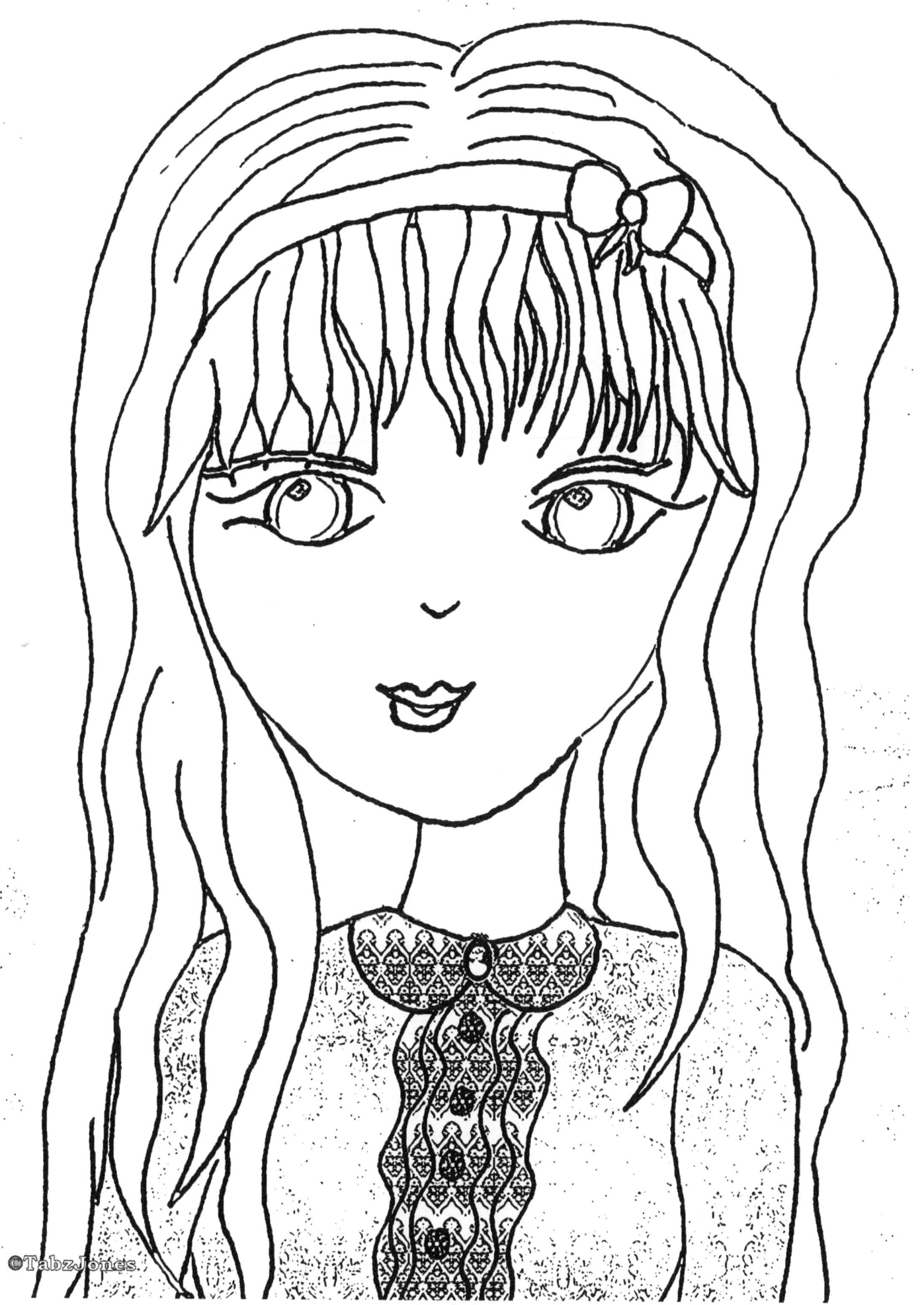

©TabzJones.

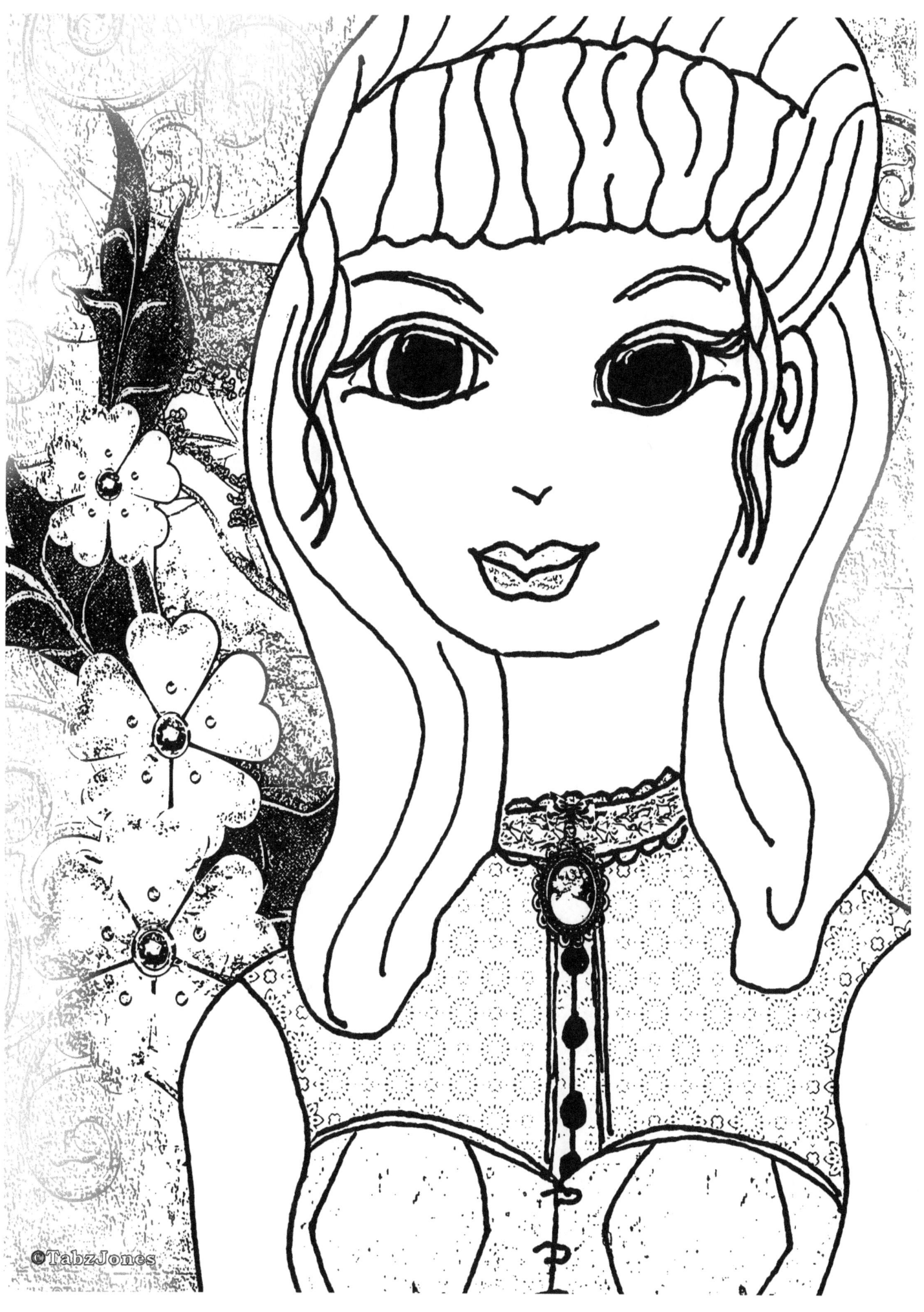

©TabzJones

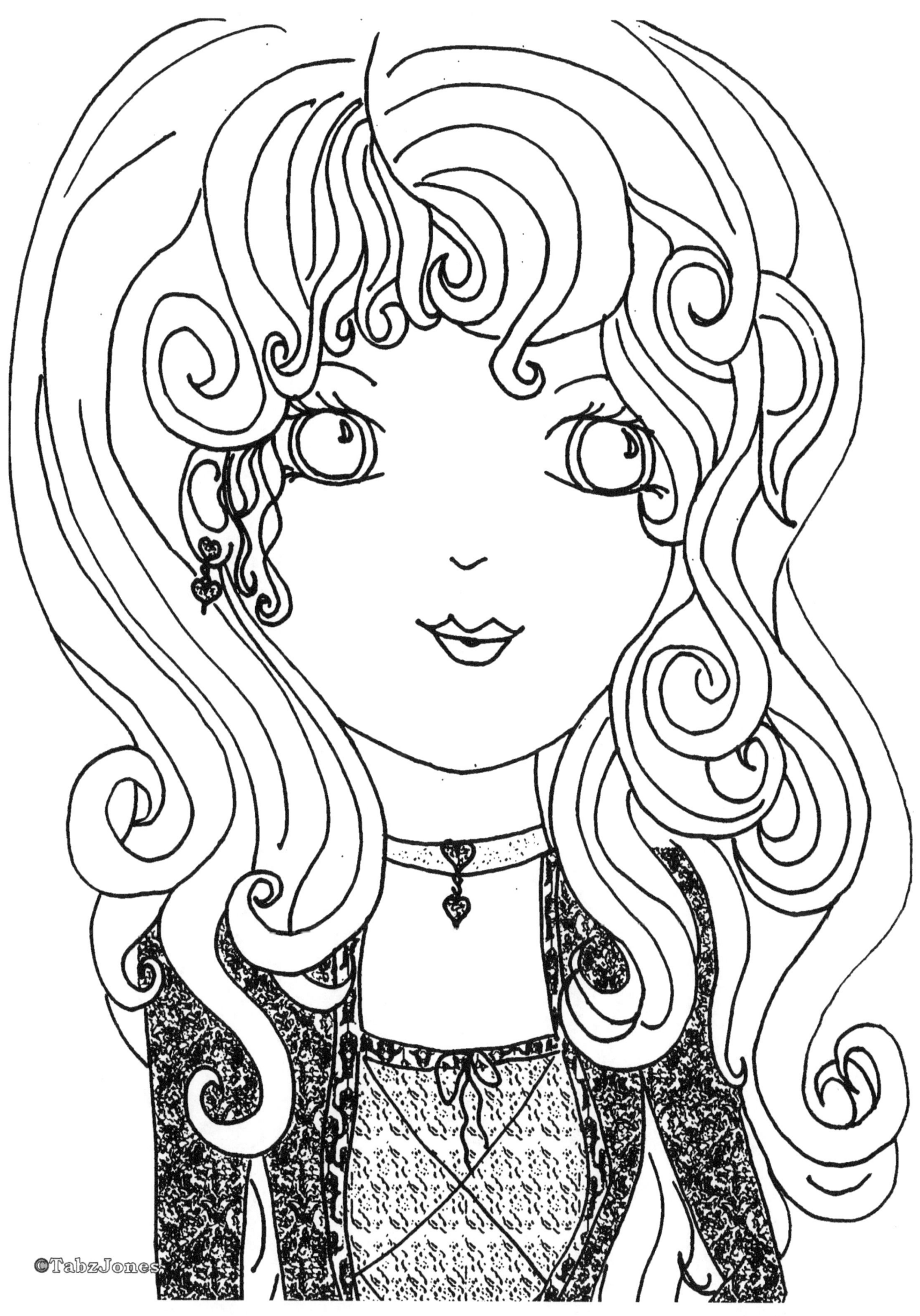

©TabzJones

Thank you

for your purchase!

To see the full catalog of my art, don't forget
to stop by
www.gothictoggs.net

www.ingramcontent.com/pod-product-compliance
Lightning Source LLC
Chambersburg PA
CBHW080606190526
45169CB00007B/2908